Please Visit
www.DKSBooks.com

To order other books by this author:
1. Hinduism - Understanding, Not Merely Knowing
2. Some Misreadings, Misinterpretations and Misrepresentations of Hinduism
3. Start of Something Beautiful (Romantic Poetry)

The Magic of Madhubala

The Beauty and Her Art

The Magic of Madhubala

Author :   Dr. Dinesh Sharma

Published through SK&L Dass Publications

2019 All Rights Reserved

No parts of this publication may be reproduced, stored in a retrieval system or transmitted in any form by any means, electronic, mechanical, photocopying, recording or otherwise without the prior permission of the author and the publisher. Copyright process in the works.

ISBN number 978-1-947711-04-4

Printed in USA by Blurb Inc.

Blurb's BookWright tool provided the layout designs and the graphic elements. The author and the publisher retain sole rights to their contributions towards this book.

www.DKSBooks.com

A Word About This Book

I have an uncanny feeling that the seed for this book was first planted in my mind the day Madhubala died in 1969 at the young age of 36. Still in my teens, the full gravity of her death did not strike me with full force at the time but the prospect of not getting to see a paragon of beauty like her in any forthcoming movies, did distress my friends and I no end. Much later in life I realized that it was not us alone who found it hard to forget her but almost everyone who knew her or her movies. Around the same time, that ancient seed started to germinate and grow. I sought after and watched as many as possible of Madhubala's movies, the research becoming easier as time went on with the advent of Internet. Converting my research into a book form still took many long years but, eventually, here we are. The book is in your hands and represents my humble tribute to a most remarkable person and artist, though I do realize that it is near impossible to do full justice to her incredible beauty, her brilliant acting and for immense humanity.

I would like to acknowledge and thank my niece Rina Puri, who untiringly helped and inspired me.

Other books by the same author available at **dksbooks.com**
1. Hinduism - understanding, not merely knowing
2. Misreadings, Misinterpretations and Misrepresentations of Hinduism
3. Start of Something Beautiful (Romantic Poetry)

Contents

Chapter 1: Madhubala - The Beauty and Her Art — 9

Chapter 2: A Short Biographical Sketch — 12

Chapter 3: Paradoxes of Madhubala's Film Career — 13

Chapter 4: The Art of Acting and Madhubala — 15
 - Believability
 - Beyond predictability
 - Sense of timing
 - Body language
 - Ability to connect with the audience
 - Comparison with compatriots
 - Ability to display feelings
 - Diction and dialog delivery
 - Dancing skills
 - Versatility
 - X-factor or charisma

Chapter 5: Madhubala's Movies and Her Performances Year to Year — 28

Chapter 6: Ranking Madhubala's Movies and Performances — 60
 - Ranking of Madhubala's own performances
 - Ranking of Madhubala's best movies
 - Ranking of Madhubala's best romantic songs
 - Ranking of Madhubala's best screen characters

Chapter 1: Madhubala – The Beauty and Her Art

Madhubala, in her short life, became a legend of epic proportions.

That Madhubala was the most elegant and good-looking woman to grace the Indian movie scene is readily accepted by most people in the know. To those who pay close attention to things, the above statement continues to hold true even if its scope is stretched into the larger stage of the world cinema, and its chronology stretched all the way to the earliest times when the photographs first started being snapped and the snapshots being stored. She was staggeringly beautiful. Many called her an incarnation of goddess Venus, some even insisting that 'Madhubala' be entered into the dictionaries as another word for beauty. Her elevation to such lofty pedestal came not only from the general movie going public but also the critics, journalists, movie makers, directors, her co-workers of all shades and grades, and almost everyone else who came across her in image or person.

One movie journalist said that '… they do not make entrancing faces like Madhubala's anymore'. One cameraman gushed '… any camera that fails to caress that captivating face would be guilty of a grave crime'. Still another one chimed '… You could photograph her from any angle without makeup and still come away with a masterpiece. She was a cameraman's delight'.

Her sublime looks inspired much poetry in filmdom and outside. One of her famous female costars said of her that '… she was ecstatically, exasperatingly beautiful'. Another called Madhubala a dream and that she was perfect from head to toe. In terms of the exquisiteness of beauty and cleanliness of features, comparisons were often made between her and Marilyn Monroe but to the connoisseurs of beauty, Marilyn Monroe was gorgeous and had a radiant appearance like Madhubala but had neither Madhubala's stately looks, nor her expressive eyes, nor her imperial presence.

The freshness of her beauty, the glow of her angelic face and the captivating power of her expressive eyes blended so well with her super-charming most-winsome smile, her disarmingly fetching demeanor and her enchantingly heartwarming personality that one look from her was enough to floor most men, almost invariably at their first sight of her. In fact, so besotted have most men been with Madhubala that almost 50 years after her death, Madhubala's popularity as an epitome of exceptional beauty continues to grow and grow and grow. Indian and international movie screens and the world at large has seen hundreds of women of extraordinary talent and pulchritude but not one has come close to matching the Madhubala magic. Even women have, by and large, found it impossible not to be affected by Madhubala's mesmerizing beauty.

Although she was extremely photogenic and the camera seemed to love her, she was even more attractive in her real life as attested by more than a few of her close acquaintances. A highly respected journalist, who was also a close family friend (BK Karanjia), emphatically stated that none of her published pictures did quite the justice to her extraordinary beauty. Dev Anand, her leading man in no less than 8 movies, expressed similar sentiments '... her singular beauty was even more radiant in real life than could ever be on the screen'. Another costar Minu Mumtaz reminisced that '... Madhubala's complexion was so fair and translucent that when she ate Paan, you could almost see the red color going down her throat'. Shammi Kapoor admits to being so dumbstruck by her beauty when he first saw her as to have become completely tongue-tied. Shashi Kapoor described her thus '...had a porcelain beauty, like Dresden china, very fragile and very delicate with a gorgeous infectious smile and very expressive eyes'. Some had a hard time believing that she was human, one famous actress even wondering if she was '...an apparition, this angel in human shape'.

Filmfare magazine wrote '... Her complexion was moon kissed and the smile an irresistible come-hither but stay-where-you-are smile. Manmohan Desai, a famous director echoed all of the above with comments like '... She was the only true beauty to grace Indian screen and she was beautiful in every film with no exceptions'.

But this book is not about Madhubala's alluring beauty or majestic appearance regarding which enough has been written. I, actually, wanted to avoid this topic altogether since it tends to distract from her masterful acting abilities, which is what this book is meant to be about. But this matter of Madhubala's beauty is so compelling that it is almost impossible to evade it altogether anytime her name comes up. It is, after all, an essential part of her mystique and overall identity. That is why I decided to get it out of the way right in the beginning. I am sure, however, that much as I might try, it is going to keep popping up here and there even in the succeeding parts of the book.

This book is not about her personal life either which has also been the topic of considerable interest and the subject of several books.

Nor is it about an unfortunate health ailment caused by a kind of congenital heart disease, which resulted in the premature termination of her young life.

Instead this book is an evaluation of her attainments as an actress who rose to be the epitome of artistic talent, besides being a marvel of divine physical endowment. She entered the movies as a child with no lessons, no formal training and no experience. As it turned out, however, she was blessed with lots of raw talent, instinctive intelligence and common savvy. She also had the humility to listen and try to understand and learn. She appreciated that a born artist though she was, in order to be a supreme professional she must enhance her inner genius and pour that extra bit of herself into her work. The quality and the brilliance of Madhubala's professional output is a living testimonial to her diligence, her meticulousness, her attention to detail, her capacity to listen and learn, her tremendous will to succeed, her readiness to accept responsibilities and her ability to apply herself to her task. Her own contribution towards boosting her fabulous God-given gifts has been acknowledged and acclaimed by the people who knew her and those who understand the art of acting

Her genius as an actor and an artist has not, however, received the attention it deserves. I have always felt that the extraordinary dexterity with which she wielded her God-given acting talents warrants a much closer examination and much greater deliberation. The accolades bestowed on her captivating physical attributes and her admirable qualities as a human being have been aplenty. They have been talked and written about. They have also been discussed, debated, dissected and raved about ceaselessly and with great ardor. But when it comes to her elemental skills as an actress and how well she employed them, the appreciation is there but the volume of the dossiers thins out substantially. This book is an attempt to remove this glitch from the narratives chronicling the life story of one of our most beloved icons. She richly merits it.

Chapter 2: A Short Biographical Sketch

Madhubala was born Mumtaz Jehan Begum on Valentine's Day, the 14th of February, 1933. Part of a loving family, she was, however, forced to seek employment as a child actor (movie Basant in 1942) to supplement her parents' tenuous financial resources. Soon she became the main breadwinner of her family that consisted of six sisters in addition to her parents. As a result, she did six movies as a child between 1942 and 1946 failing, however, to get much schooling.

As she was good-looking, honest and hard-working, offers for grown up roles started pouring in as soon as she reached the pubertal age. Barely 13, she was initiated into the movies as the leading lady of Neel Kamal, released in 1947.

The success of Neel Kamal opened the floodgates and she appeared in 4 more movies in 1947 itself, all of them as their female lead. She was received well by the public and the next couple of years pushed her to the top rungs of Indian filmdom. She made those top rungs emphatically her own for the entire decade of 1950s becoming, in the process, one of the biggest ever darlings of Indian Cinema.

Unfortunately, around the end of the 1950s decade, she started suffering the clinical effects of a congenital (born with it) heart disease - most probably either an Atrial or a Ventricular Septal Defect - which was incurable in those days. Poor health forced declining productivity (quantitatively, not qualitatively) so much so that she was barely able to work in the 1960s. Eventually the disease, progressing inexorably, claimed her life at the agonizingly young age of thirty six in 1969, leaving grieving millions. She had been able to work effectively only till 1960 when she had barely reached the age of 27 or 28, a fact that emphasizes how remarkable her achievements were relative to her age.

She was immensely popular with men and was repeatedly approached with requests for marriage. She did have a short affair with one of the eminent male actors of the time, Dilip Kumar, but for several reasons it did not materialize into anything more tangible or long-term. She did eventually marry another film personality, the famous singer-actor Kishore Kumar, towards the end of her career but it proved to be an unhappy marriage. Perhaps her declining physical health had something to do with that. Despite brave efforts in the last few years of her life to revive her movie career, she was unable to beat her illness.

Chapter 3: Paradoxes of Madhubala's Film Career

There is a general feeling that in spite of Madhubala's undeniable physical charms, her considerable acting prowess and her intense popularity, **her movies did not do as well at the box office as one would expect.** Out of a total of 67 movies as the adult female lead, barely 15 or so are considered to be runaway successes. Although her own performance as an artist and an enchantress never fell below par, such frequency of flops did indeed become a cause for alarm in the circles close to her in mid-1950s. On the surface, it certainly does appear to be an anomaly which warrants a review.

Then there is another paradox that falls under the same general category as 'professional oddities'. Most critics and experts have unreservedly vouched for Madhubala's having possessed exceptional gifts as an actress. But despite glowing encomiums and standing ovations from the critics, she ended up awfully **short of acting awards and decorations.** Although it is commonly conceded that the correlation between awards and excellence is hardly ever concordant or proportionate, the very extent of aberration in this case raises serious questions meriting scrutiny.

On careful analysis, several factors appear to account for this disconcerting anomaly.

1. Both her father, as her professional manager, and Madhubala herself deserve equal criticism for their **failure to properly select the roles** she was going to play. Too many of her movies were poorly conceived, poorly written, poorly directed and suffered from the added burden of poor production values. Also, an inordinately large number of them lacked a leading man of stature. Anyone with an iota of common sense would have foreseen such films to be box office disasters even before they went to the floor. Then again, hardly any movies she selected had the kind of characters, story-lines or production values that would predispose their actors to win major awards (Mughal-e-Azam can be cited as an exception but it came in 1960, near the end of Madhubala's career). We all know that there is a natural predilection for the awards to flow in the direction of a certain kinds of roles, nature of the roles being at least as important as to how they are played.

The blame for this appalling selection has been laid at many doors, none more than at Madhubala's own, her personal and domestic financial compulsions forcing her and her father to make shortsighted decisions. A family that valued financial security as much as theirs - with justifiable reasons, of course - could hardly decline another infusion of money that another signed contract would bring. Financial compulsions apart, poor judgment and plain lack of foresight probably played a significant role as well.

2. Another failing pertains to her **father's disagreeable personality and poor skills as a professional manager,** a job that he did with great gusto but with little finesse. Madhubala is said to have lost many excellent roles for this reason.

3. Another way Madhubala herself is thought to have contributed to this lapse is **by being too nice** and thus unable to inflict the pain of rejection on her prospective producers. Some of her more crappy movies were the result of their acceptance by her as a return of past favors done to her by their makers, gratitude being her sole motive. Such misplaced sense of obligation made her overlook the ill effects of her own largess on her career.

4. **The blinding glare of her radiant personality and alluring beauty** is often cited as a major factor in distracting the attention of viewers from her artistry and work. People used to be in such a thrall looking at her that they forgot to pay heed to how she was performing as an actress.

This explanation sounded rather flaky until we tested it ourselves. Watching her movies with friends, they would not stop harping on Madhubala's good looks even when specifically asked to limit themselves to her acting and acting alone. Repeated reminders did not seem to help much either. Their enamored and distracted state was not hard to see.

Even those movies in which Madhubala's acting performance is generally acknowledged to be of the highest caliber as in Mr. and Mrs. 55, Tarana, Amar, Mughal-e-Azam, Kala Pani', Insaan Jaag Utha etc., people don't seem to notice it without repeated cues and reminders. So captivated do they become by her beauty and her smiles that those are the only things that seem to register. Often they have to make a conscious effort to propel themselves away from her beauty and towards her acting. Once that happens, of course, the adulations for her acting flow as freely as for her beauty.

Chapter 4: The Art of Acting and Madhubala

In this chapter, we will consider some of the essentials of good acting with reference to Madhubala where relevant, giving examples from her movies. An analysis of where and how her performances fit into a particular acting element will also be made. Some of the comments made in this section could possibly be repeated later, albeit in a different context, when we discuss her memorable movie scenes in the next chapter of this book.

A. Believability

While acting, an actor or actress is portraying a character which is different from him or herself but he or she must accurately represent the way this character is written in context of the screenplay. The character itself may be imaginary but the actor must make it real. She must be convincing and believable although, quite understandably, an actor can be only as realistic as the character that has been written by its creator. The 'believability' in this context means that the actor does not have to make an unreal character real but must portray it in a plausibly persuasive manner.

It takes imagination, intelligence and the ability to properly visualize and interpret an imaginary character's true nature and personality. It requires an actor to observe keenly and listen well. Fortunately, for Madhubala, she had oodles of these virtues intrinsically built into her constitution so well, in fact, as to be almost her second nature. During her career she played all kinds of screen roles, some written very well others not quite so, but she never appeared to have any trouble in interpreting or adopting herself to everyone of them. She could slip into any one of them with utmost ease and adopt its persona incredibly well. Movies like Howrah Bridge, Kal Hamara Hai (especially the bad sister part), Mehlon Ke Khwaab, Half ticket and Gateway of India had her playing with distinction such roles as were far removed from her own personality.

This ability to visualize, interpret and internalize made 'believability' one of the strongest fortes of Madhubala's acting and, as a result, she developed a reputation for her ability to maintain a perfect balance between the various traits of her characters' personalities without underplaying or overplaying any. So much so that many writers and directors of her movies expressed open admiration for her capacity to make their characters more real and lifelike than even they had visualized.

B. Beyond predictability

Most top actors end up working in scores of movies. Becoming predictable and stereotypical is an almost unavoidable occupational hazard and can be a real downer for the viewing public. We have seen this malady afflict the best of them - Raj Kapoor, Dev Anand, Shammi Kapoor, Nargis, Meena Kumari and Nutan. Even Dilip Kumar and Vijayantimala with all their versatility and range were accused of it. Madhubala managed to be an exception though, and for good reasons. To start with, her own personality was naturally untainted by mannerisms. And then, Madhubala like most great actors, made a conscious effort to prevent the implantation into her own personality and tagging along of the traits, mannerisms, quirks and affectations of the characters she played. Was she more successful than others due to her simplicity, her uncomplicated personality, her lack of ego or was it simply a case of another one of God's gifts, we will never know.

This also explains why every movie and every performance of Madhubala's could present her in a fresh new light, and why not losing the 'surprise element' was to prove one of her strongest suits.

C. Sense of timing

'The exact moment' is a very important ingredient in the art of acting. Exactly when a certain gesture unfolds, a smile makes its appearance, a word escapes the lips and a tear flows down the eyes, can dramatically affect the impact and potency of a scene.

Madhubala picked up a splendid reputation for her unerring timing in comic situations as movies like Tarana, Mr. and Mrs. 55 and Chalti Ka Naam Gaadi prove. But in sentimental, poignant and dramatic passages too her sense of timing was no less authoritative. One of our favorite scenes is the little smile she flashes in the beginning of the song '...mere sapne men' in the the movie Rajhath as she looks back and notices her friend watching.

D. Body language

Madhubala could employ the movements and gestures of her head, hands, fingers and her gait - in effect, the entire body - in a remarkably eloquent manner in expressing her thoughts and emotions, while staying within the limits imposed by believability. One of her directors said that there was sheer artistry in her movements, a purity of actions and expressions.

We saw examples of her exquisite use of body language, the way she moved, the way she threw her head and the way she motioned her hands in practically every one of her movies but Tarana, Insaan Jaag Utha, Mughal-e-Azam, Saiyan, Badal, Mr. and Mrs. 55, Chalti Ka Naam Gaadi, Gateway of India, Howrah Bridge, Barsaat Ki Raat and Mehlon Ke Khwab are the most spectacular examples.

E. Ability to connect with the audience

The ultimate worth of an actress or actor is essentially measured by the kind of impression she leaves on her audience. Madhubala knew she was beautiful and that her fans knew it. But she was also aware that to be irresistible she must portray her characters well. So she made sure that she was compelling in everyone of her portrayals whether naughty and amusing or somber and melancholic. And her robust and enduring impact on her viewers is emphatically supported by history.

F. Comparisons with compatriots

Comparisons, they say, are odious but they do provide a wonderful parameter to gauge disparate entities (with caveats, of course). The problem is that the comparisons, despite their admitted efficacy, often require inexact juxtaposing of the entities being compared inviting rejections like the proverbial apples and oranges analogy. Our observations here are, therefore, of a general nature and not intended to be exhaustive or absolute.

Another thing, we are going to stick to Madhubala's contemporary times. Different time periods introduce additional variables making the comparisons even less workable or reliable. Very few of the actors and actresses of later times can, in any case, be contrasted against Madhubala because most have not achieved a commensurate level of credentials. None of the excellent actors like Samita Patil, Shabana Azmi, Om Puri, Nasiruddin Shah were the popular phenomena that Madhubala was. On the other hand, most popular actors of the post-Madhubala years can not claim proportionate acting credentials. Amitabh Bachchan and

Madhuri Dixit are perhaps the only ones who can be considered both good and popular.

Under such conditions, therefore, a synchronous compatriot comparison is more likely to be meaningful.

Her Male contemporaries

The most competent top-level male actors of Madhubala's time were Ashok Kumar, Raj Kapoor, Dilip Kumar, Dev Anand and Sunil Dutt. **Dilip Kumar,** arguably, was the best of the lot. In those male dominated times, he was said to monopolize the screen with most of his heroines. Not with Madhubala though, as she proved to be too good even for him (in some movies, Vyjayanthimala could be considered another exception). They worked together in four movies and she outshone him in every one of them. Both were excellent in **Tarana** but it was Madhubala who left on the minds of the viewers the strongest images not only of instant gratification but also of long-lasting memories. In **Sangdil**, she played an angel-like person who, however, is torn by conflicting emotions and circumstances beyond her control. Dilip Kumar played a passionate but selfish and frustrated man. Although both of them were equally convincing in their roles, Madhubala brought a certain freshness to her role which Dilip Kumar could not. Her interpretation of the role and its presentation, her body language and her emoting were innovative, immaculate and very convincing whereas Dilip Kumar's mannerisms and style came across as stale, almost stereotypical for him. In **Amar**, both were exceptional in the happy early parts of the movie, but in the later or the troubled portions, she outdistanced Dilip Kumar by a country mile. She showed the ability to express a motley mixture of emotions with competence and assurance that he could not. In the same frame you could see on her face (and her eyes) the feelings of surprise, dejection, love, concern, apprehension, wistfulness, defeat and acceptance, all almost simultaneously (the song '… na shikva hai koi' is an example). The story of the movie provided Dilip Kumar, too, the opportunity to show all of the above, plus the added spice of guilt but all we ever saw was a display of dejection and avoidance on an almost immobile face. We tried to detect at least some love, desire, the dread of losing everything or even guilt in his portrayal but none ever materialized, not simultaneously, not even sequentially. In **Mughal-e-Azam,** Madhubala's performance was simply supreme and Dilip Kumar's not even in the frame. Any comparisons between the two in this movie don't even deserve to be contemplated.

Raj Kapoor was an extremely talented actor who did not always perform up to his potential. He worked with Madhubala in several movies in the beginning of their careers including Neel Kamal, the debut film for both. Most others are not available but as far as **Neel Kamal** is concerned, the lively portrayal of a blithe and innocent girl by Madhubala proved to be the movie's high point. In **Dil Ki Rani**, both of them were adorable but it was Madhubala who won the popularity stakes with her ebullient, engaging personality and fluid acting. Many years later, they appeared together again in **Do Ustad**. Both were delightful in this mediocre movie, with not much to choose between the two, although Madhubala's beauty and vivaciousness made her, as always, the scene stealer.

She formed, with **Dev Anand**, the lead pair in no less than eight movies. None out of these, other than **Kala Pani**, can be considered to be of outstanding merit. In it, both played their roles with skill and empathy. While Madhubala had many memorable scenes in which she excelled, Dev Anand matched her with perhaps his best performance to date. Their other movies together were average fare with not much to write about but due to her unaffected, spirited and stimulating performances she almost always managed to leave a greater impression than him on the movie viewing public (except maybe in **Sharabi**, in which both were equally good). Dev Anand was rather passive and unimpressive in his early years as exemplified by his performances in movies like **Nirala** and **Aaram**.

Ashok Kumar was a natural actor and played his roles with studied ease. He could be very effective without having to manipulate the viewers' attention. Madhubala also had all those attributes but had, in addition, those streaks of brilliance and was so much easier on the eye. She could dazzle and easily dominate. That is why their movies together **Mahal, Howrah Bridge, Chalti Ka Naam Gaadi and Ek Saal** are remembered for Madhubala's performances and not Ashok Kumar's, although he was his usual competent self.

Her Female contemporaries

Nargis, Nutan, Vyjayanthimala, and Meena Kumari

This was a period of time in Indian movies when a whole bevy of actresses could pack a powerful acting punch. There was a surfeit of genius as well as accomplishment. These four would be good for our comparisons since they symbolize, besides Madhubala, the absolute finest of the lot. I understand that we are excluding fantastic actresses like Suraiya, Kamini Kaushal, Nalini Jaywant, Geeta Bali, Waheeda Rehman, Mala Sinha, Bina Rai and Sharmila Tagore from this list but most people will agree that, purely from an acting standpoint, they belong in a second tier just below the top 5 mentioned above.

There is very little to choose amongst the top five. Madhubala probably scored over others in terms of charisma and personality. Versatility was her forte as well but the same can be said of **Nutan** and **Vyjayanthimala**. Actually Vyjayanthimala's superlative skills in dancing gave her a leg up on everyone else. **Meena Kumari, Nutan and Nargis's** outstanding judgment in selecting artistically meaningful and socially relevant roles brought them great awards and accolades. It must be said to their credit that they did execute their roles breathtakingly well and richly deserved them. Madhubala scored over them by being the least stereotyped and predictable, although the same could justifiably be said about Vyjayanthimala as well.

One area in which she simply surpassed every other was the adroit manner in which she could express multiple emotions in the same frame. Everyone of the top 5 mentioned above was a past master in expressing emotions but a close scrutiny shows that it was one emotion at a time. The emotions could follow each other quickly but it was always only one per any given moment. Madhubala could, however, bring an assortment of emotions to light up her face almost simultaneously. We will have examples later as we move along the book.

G. Ability to display feelings

The ability to express emotions specific to the requirements of the script with conviction and with just the required amount of dramatics is a basic essential for every actor. A genuine actor will make the audience believe in the sentiments she portrays and will completely lose herself in the feelings of the character and their context in the movie. In discussing Madhubala's ability to portray feelings, let us pick one emotion at a time.

1. Comedy

Comedy does not always bring joy or even laughter to the viewer. It can be enjoyable but it can also fall flat or worse. It can even make one cry if it is poorly done. Good comedy should not only be more than mere clownishness or buffoonery, it must also go beyond mere display of joy, happiness, energy, effervescence, flirtatiousness, banter, fun and frolic. It must have an extra something to have superior entertainment value. Poorly conceived or performed it can be irritating and even disgusting.

Even well-written and well scripted comedies need considerable help from the actors involved to make them genuinely amusing. Some people are of the opinion that it is much harder to impress in a comic than a serious role. What is the quality of an actor's giggle, chuckle, guffaw or the smile? Did the naughty interludes evoke the thrills and excitement they were meant to? Was the flirtatiousness seductive without being titillating or vulgar? Did the actor's exuberance light up the screen without going over-the-top? The sense of timing is even more important in comedy scenes than in most others. Actors need to understand comedy well in all its subtleties and nuances. For all these reasons, most actors consider playing a comic role to be the litmus test of their acting skills.

Coming to Madhubala, this was one aspect of acting in which she won almost unanimous approbation. She consistently aced every comic requirement outlined in the previous paragraph. Reputedly blessed with a natural flair for comedy, she could actually be quite sublime. She relished comedy and it showed. In comic roles, whether it was a few sundry scenes in a movie like Nirala, Badal or Kala Pani) or almost continuous as in Tarana, Mr. and Mrs. 55, Chalti Ka Naam Gaadi, Gateway of India, Mehlon Ke Khwab and Half Ticket, she could easily outclass all other top actresses and actors of her time. It is difficult to imagine anyone else in her place in most of her movies but in comedies, it is impossible. Her mere presence on the screen was a veritable mood elevator.

2. Happiness and contentment

The display of happiness is different from being hilarious and funny but they can and often do coexist. Madhubala could manage portraying cool pleasure, contentment and bliss as easily as the laughter, energy and even the boisterousness of comedy. For one thing, she happened to have the coolest smile in the world. The writers run out of epithets in describing her smile even before they do in describing her beauty. While her smile could, by itself, project the ambiance that all is well with the world, she had the uncanny knack of amplifying its effect manifold by simply turning on the mastery of her facial expressions and body language. Lots of movies gave Madhubala this opportunity and the result was always exhilarating and often electrifying. Some of our most favorite scenes of her portraying elation and bliss are from Beqasoor, Tarana, Badal, Saiyan, Barsaat Ki Raat, Howrah Bridge, Phagun and Insaan Jaag Utha.

3. Sadness and grief

Meena Kumari was called the queen of tragedy. Nutan was in no way less competent in displaying various nuances of tragedy. In fact all of the top actresses were darn good at it. We do not know if it is because deep down dejection and despondence are relatively easy emotions to express on the screen.

But what distinguished Madhubala was the way she could emote sorrow and grief without too many tears and facial contortions. She never needed to be melodramatic. All she needed was to conjure up that shadow of mournful gloom in her intense eyes - something only she could with such powerful conviction - and it would look as if her heart were exploding in from anguish and despair.

Here again, the media appear to have been too focused on her looks or her comic genius to notice her dexterity in emoting sadness, desperation, defeat, rejection and repressed anger until she forced everyone to sit up and take notice in Mughal-e-Azam. She had impressively executed grim and funereal scenes in movies like Apradhi, Nirala, Tarana, Shirin Farhad, Sangdil etc. too but the most unforgettable one for us is from Naata while singing "…dekhte dekhte jal gaya". We are yet to see any other pair of eyes express the feeling of extreme loss, abysmal helplessness and the impending doom as hers did (and that includes those of Meena Kumari, Nutan and Dilip Kumar). Her eyes could simply tear the viewer hearts asunder. Similar descriptions apply to her renditions of Nirala songs '….mehfil men jal uthi shama' and ' …Jo dil ko jalaye sataye', as also the Amar song ' …Jaane wale se mulakat'.

4. Love and devotion

Madhubala was magnificent in love scenes. So uniquely convincing was she in romantic situations that almost invariably the viewers mistook her to be madly and actually in love with whichever male costar she was working with. She would conjure such wistful intensity in her eyes, such facial appearances and such body language that it was hard to believe that her love was only acting. And she could always look like a dream in these scenes. We have heard people say that Madhubala was a PhD in the science of the screen chemistry of love. To be profoundly convinced, one only has to see the relevant scenes from Insaan Jaag Utha (the songs '…baat badhti gayi' and '…chand sa mukhra', and her conversations with Sunil Dutt just prior to both), Barsat Ki Raat (song '…zindagi bhar nahin'), Passport (song '…saaz-e-dil'), Phagun (song "…main soya akhiyaan meeche) and Tarana (practically the whole movie). More examples are listed in the penultimate section of the last chapter of this book

5. Passion

Madhubala's was an era when displaying emotions like passion and lust on screen were very much scoffed at especially when it came to the leading ladies. But the few times subtle shades of passion and desire made it to the screen in Madhubala's movies, she gave their portrayal such a wistful immediacy that they became the stuff of the legend. Dev Anand and Madhubala's meeting on the roof of her house in Kala Pani was one such instance. Another memorable one was in Mr. and Mrs. 55, when she and Guru Dutt break into the song '…udhar tum haseen ho' as the desirability of spousal love dawns on her.

The manner in which her expressions and body kinesics could enunciate pent-up passions, had the ability to make the viewer almost sweat with tension, but it was always done with great finesse, decorum, poise and understated dignity.

6. Innocence and vulnerability

Most heroines of Indian screen have capably played victims of circumstances but can anyone match the guiltless innocence and the helpless vulnerability of Madhubala in Neel Kamal, Ek Saal, Naata, Apradhi, Tarana, Barsaat Ki Raat, Beqasoor and, of course, Mughal-e-Azam.

7. Ada

Ada is an Urdu word for which an exact English equivalent is hard to find. Probably best defined as a demeanor which is a blend of softness, style and manner, often but not always incorporating mild flirtatiousness which teases and entices. Ada is most popularly employed in its positive connotations. And this positivity is certainly applicable to the Adas that were part of Madhubala's screen persona. They came to be recognized as important ingredients of her famous charm. Combined with her physical beauty and glorious smiles, her Adas were capable of generating a constant stream of magnetism and electricity.

8. Arrogance and haughtiness

She played an impetuous and snobbish woman as the 'affected' sister in Kal Hamara Hai but insecurity, vulnerability and naivete were also essential components of this character. Combining them all could have been artistically exacting but she took it all in her stride and came out with flying colors as has been universally acknowledged by the critics. How she could make a seriously negative character so lovable despite its hauteur, conceit and villainy can only be explained on the basis of Madhubala's magic touch. In Mr. and Mrs. 55, in another memorable performance, she portrayed the elegant imperiousness of a rich heiress with a delightful doze of callow sweetness.

9. Anger and outbursts

Although not components of her own personality and also rarely visible in her screen incarnations, she was called upon to enact a display of insolence and anger once in a while. The scene in Instant Haag Utah in which she slaps Sunni Mutt in misplaced anger and the one in Kala Pan in which she tells Dev Aland to get out, were perfectly enacted by Madhubala with just the right doze of indignation, annoyance, exasperation and fury.

10. Other intense emotions

Madhubala was a past-master at expressing many other intense emotions like being distressed, agitated, hateful or scared. There were numerous occasions for her to display her dexterity at these in relevant screen situations. We love the encounter between her and Dilip Kumar in Tarawa soon after he runs away from his wedding towards the end of the movie. She portrayed a lot of emotions in those 2 or 3 minutes and was simply marvelous in enacting every one of them.

The other favorites include her reaction when Dilip Kumar informs her in the same movie of his impending departure to visit his home and when, in Mr. and Mrs. 55, she runs into Guru Dutt at the club and he tries to placate her. These were flawless in execution, Madhubala being absolutely brilliant. Her adroitly enacted display of all these emotions in some of Madhubala's encounters with Prithviraj Kapoor in Mughal-e-Azam has gained her an acclaim of almost mythical proportions and needs no emphasis here. Particularly impressive was the way she made her pain and fear so palpable as to almost force the audience scream from anguish. She was also extremely convincing in scenes such as when Om Parkash brandishes a knife at her in Gateway of India; when she stumbles into the deranged wife of Dilip Kumar in Sangdill; when she is woken up by an 'intruder' in her bedroom in Chalti Ka Naam Gadi and when she sees a snake in Do Ustad.

11. The ability to portray complex emotions

Expressing any emotion in a convincing manner is an achievement by itself but a human being can be going through several thoughts and emotions at the same time. The mind can think faster than the facial muscles can respond and follow. Expressing a medley of thoughts and emotions flowing in a constant stream requires, therefore, an almost superhuman effort.

We have diligently watched all the actors and actresses for this particular acting characteristic and have hardly if ever noticed anyone, except Madhubala, to effectively display more than two emotions in the same frame. We have already mentioned two examples from the movies Tarawa in section 10, above) and Mar in the section comparing her with Filip Kumar. I would like to mention a third one, the one which has her singing the '... jab pray sukiyaki to song in Maugham-e-Assam. It's a treat to watch her bringing out every shade of love and resentment; dignity and defiance; vulnerability and fear; hope and foreboding, all of them topped with oodles of grace, elegance and beauty and all almost simultaneously. This was a class act without parallel, at least in Indian cinema.

H. Diction and dialog delivery

It seems like Madhubala's genius encompassed every aspect of the art of acting, leaving practically nothing out.

Most roles require an actor to speak the normal everyday speech. Not only did Madhubala have a clear and pleasant voice, she knew how to modulate its pitch, tonality, accent and resonance to fit the situation, using pauses and inflections very capably without ever sounding unnatural or over dramatic.

Some roles require unconventional peculiarities of elocution. They presented no poser, however, to Madhubala as she was a fast learner. Without trouble or hesitation she could bring to her voice the required inflections and intonations, matching them perfectly to the needs of her roles as exemplified by her rustic girl roles in Naata, Tarana, Phagun and Pardes and her sophisticated urbanites in Amar, Jhumroo, Kala Paani, Passport, Do Ustad and Ek Saal. One particularly demanding case was that of the courtesan in Mughal-e-Azam requiring her to speak a specifically cultivated language, in a particularly refined tone and style. She also delivered with distinction her dialogs in Bhojpuri in Insaan Jaag Utha; Anglo-Indian accent in Howrah Bridge; the Maharashtrian street language in Gateway of India and the whimsical quasi-poetical dialect in Dil Ki Rani.

I. Dancing skills

Dancing by itself is not an acting skill but in Indian movies it is almost obligatory as a part of the overall package because most of them contain dance and song sequences as their essential components. Madhubala had absolutely no dancing background. So she took a few lessons and worked on it.

She never became a master but she was at least as good as the other top actresses of her time except, of course, Vyjayanthimala who, as we know, was a peerless trained dancer. In Madhubala's favor, however, were her alluring figure and the intrinsic rhythm of her body which made her dancing look pleasing to the eye. Many dance sequences in those days involved a simple swaying motion and she was absolutely heavenly in those, so much so that in movies like Dulari, Beqasoor, Saiyan, Pardes, Badal, Rail Ka Dibba, Howrah Bridge and Mughal-e-Azam, her acting was not the only one that won her rich plaudits. Her dancing enthused the audience and the critics alike.

J. Versatility

Madhubala's ability to portray different characters and competently display all types of emotions was noted and recognized very early in her career. Motilal, her costar and a highly accomplished actor himself said during the shooting of Hanste Aansoo, a 1950s movie, that '…the versatility of this girl seems to be endless'.

This early promise received plenty of corroboration from the remarkable diversity of roles that she so deftly pulled off in later years and in different genres and styles. Out of the top acting echelons of Indian filmdom, Vyjayanthimala was the only one who displayed comparable versatility. Madhubala scored over Vyjayanthimala in comic roles and Vyjayanthimala outdid Madhubala in dancing abilities.

K. X-factor or charisma

Madhubala lives on in our hearts after all these years not only for her beauty, her ability to express her characters well and her star quality but also because she had something uncanny, something intangible, something totally inexplicable in her that could fire up special sensors in our hearts and minds even when she wasn't doing anything out of the ordinary. This must be what they call 'charisma'.

Surely her beauty was staggering, her physical presence was overpowering and she owned a cornucopia of outstanding artistic talents. But her charisma made her much more than a mathematical product of these rich treasures. That she was one of the most charismatic human beings ever has made some people credit a divine hand for this special gift.

We can't vouch for such superhuman intervention but her good human qualities did elevate her above most other achievers. Not only was her conduct beyond reproach, the warmth of her personality, her inner goodness, her simplicity, her moderation, her lovable demeanor and her compassionate giving nature added to her persona an extra layer of luster and magnetism.

5: Madhubala's Movies and Her Performances Year to Year

Madhubala acted in a total of 73 movies, 6 of them as a child artist only one of which - Basant, released in the year 1942 - is readily available. Basant which also happened to be her first movie, hit the screens when she was only nine years old.

Not long afterwards, still only 13 to 14 years of age, she graduated to the grown-up lead roles in 1947 having been teamed up with Raj Kapoor, another rookie destined to become a top-notch achiever in Indian filmdom. The movie was titled Neel Kamal. After a reasonably successful debut in this movie, Madhubala made rapid strides to become one of the most popular actresses of Indian cinema and one of its biggest stars over the next 15 years or so, her most productive years stretching from 1947 to the end of the 1950s decade.

Immediately following this period, however, her productivity fell significantly. She had a grand total of 6 movies released from 1960 till her death in 1969. The major cause for this decline in numbers was her illness as mentioned in her biographical sketch. Some of these movies had already been partially shot before 1960 but still required the use of doubles for Madhubala or extensive editing to become worthy of being screened.

In the following pages we will present a rundown on those movies of Madhubala that are still available. Many, especially those from her early years, appear to have simply gone out of circulation, either destroyed or just unavailable from 'other' reasons. Occasionally a few photos of their marketing posters make their appearance here and there. One may also come across the video clips of a few songs from Nadaan and Paras. Rarely, the audio-only versions (sans videos) of a few songs from Nazneen, Teerandaz, Baghi Sipahi, Khazana and other 'unavailable' movies of hers may be heard as well.

Most of what is available can be seen on YouTube and we recommend that the reader freely use this resource to review Madhubala's movies and songs, employing the discussion below as a guide. The timings of the scenes given within the parentheses are for the respective YouTube movie videos. The movies and the song clips can be searched by typing in their titles as given in this book.

1. Year 1942

This year saw her enter the movie industry as Baby Mumtaz and taste success right away. She adopted the name Madhubala only after Neel Kamal in 1947.

Basant

In Basant, her first movie, she played the eight year old singing daughter of a separated couple. She acquitted herself well as an actor and was also hailed as a box office success. Two songs '… mere chhote se man men chhoti si' and ' …hamko hain pyari hamari galiyan' picturized on her became popular hits. While she looked cute and innocent and her acting was natural and commensurate with the situations, the portents of her coming greatness were not quite visible at this stage.

Memorable scenes

*Both the songs mentioned above.

2. Years 1944, 1945 and 1946

Madhubala continued to work as a child artist doing at least five movies (Mumtaz Mahal, Dhanna Bhagat, Pujari, Phulwari and Rajputani) during these years, last 3 in 1946 alone. None of them is available for viewing, however. We are also yet to come across a song clip from any one of them. No published comments about her acting abilities are to be found either although we did see one very positive comment about her work ethic even as a child.

3. Year 1947

Madhubala had, by this time, grown into a beautiful young girl and the producers were falling over each other in a bid to draft her into their own movies as a leading lady. Kedar Sharma won this race and she debuted in his 1947 movie 'Neel Kamal'. Its success provoked a minor deluge, 4 more of her movies materializing in quick succession in 1947 itself. While Dil Ki Rani, like Neel Kamal, established her as an excellent prospect, the other 3 Chittor Vijay, Khubsoorat Duniya and Mere Bhagwan disappeared without fanfare.

Neel Kamal

At the time of the movie's release, Madhubala was barely 14 years old but she lived up to Kedar Sharma's expectations and gave a scintillating account of herself. As a young country maiden infatuated with an artist, becoming, in the process, an unwitting rival to a princess for his attentions, she delivered a sensitive portrayal of the tender moonstruck girl who meets a tragic end. She impressed one and all.

Memorable scenes

*As a country girl, she was presented very much the ordinary girl next door but her exquisite features and captivating smile made her look more like an angel. Our favorite scene is the short conversation between her and the hero followed by the song '…kal Jamuna tat par aayoge' (49:50 - 54:00).

Dil Ki Rani

It was an interesting movie - a rather theatrical comedy full of farcical but cute situations. Raj Kapoor, its hero, spoke more than half his dialogs in verse. Though the script itself did not give opportunities for extraordinary acting, both he and Madhubala made their oddball roles quite believable and entertaining. However, call it her innocent beauty, her tasteful but understated sense of comedy or pure charisma, it was she who garnered all the accolades.

The surge in fan following that had started with Neel Kamal, accelerated with Dil ki Rani to become a veritable downpour with Mahal less than two years hence. And from then on, it has been flowing in torrents, pouring

right into the modern times despite her death almost half a century prior.

Memorable scenes

　　*The scenes in which she first meets Raj Kapoor and his friend (12:00 - 26:00) provide a good sampling of the whole movie's tempo and tenor.

4. Year 1948

Out of the 4 movies released in 1948, only Amar Prem had a front-runner, Raj Kapoor, as her male counterpart. That, however, is not the only reason why the three others - Parai Aag, Lal Dupatta and Desh Seva - flopped so miserably as to be found nowhere. No comments or reviews on them are available either.

5. Year 1949

1949 saw a spate of Madhubala movies, no less than nine of them hitting the screens. But we can talk about only 4 because the rest (Sipahiya, Paras, Neki aur Badi, Imtihaan and Daulat) have simply vanished from the circulation. In Paras, Madhubala was said to have made the veteran Kamini Kaushal 'look like an amateur'. Several Paras video song clips, including one filmed on Madhubala ('…aaj meri duniyan men') can be viewed on YouTube.

Singaar

In this movie Madhubala was pitched once again, after Paras, against a popular and established actress, Suraiya this time. She played an uncomplicated and righteous dancing girl who inadvertently becomes the 'other woman' in a love triangle. It is generally agreed that she outshone Suraiya by at least a million to one, not a mean feat for a newcomer.

Memorable scenes

　　*Two of the three songs picturized on Madhubala, '…dil aane ke dhang' and '…chanda re tu meri gawahi', both sung by Surinder Kaur, the famous Punjabi singer, were your enchantment and became extremely popular.

*We also loved the two sequences of the confrontations between Madhubala and Suraiya (1:40:10 - 1:43:12 and 2:02:10 - 2:05:15).

Dulari

Some people felt that Madhubala was excessively subdued in this movie. Some even saw this as a lack of confidence. We completely disagree with this analysis. In fact, we feel that she interpreted the role very well and played it to the hilt. After all she was supposed to be a girl kidnapped and then tyrannically abused all her life by her kidnappers. Aware that she was a caged bird, that the kidnappers' main enforcer was out to target her without mercy and that her chances of escape were practically nonexistent, her character's docile passivity was entirely legitimate. In any case, if this is how her character was written by the scriptwriter, no way could she be chirpy and perky like Gita Bali's character. We think her portrayal of her character was well-balanced and she acquitted herself extremely well.

Memorable scenes

*We loved her portrayal of complex emotions in the happy songs of this movie. While her feelings of elation and release at finding true love and its potential to free her from her bondage, emerge succinctly through her eyes and so do the deeply lurking shadows of her still desperate situation. There were several such songs but our most favorite are '…muhabbat hamari zamana hamara' and '…mil jul ke gayenge hum'.

Mahal

This was the movie that eventually eased Madhubala into the top echelons of Hindi cinema. Appearing mostly as a mysterious wraith-like presence, she impressed everyone with her bewitching, delicate, almost ethereal looks and her eloquently expressive face on which she amply and effectively displayed the gloom of unrequited desperate love and the pain of her inner anguish. Particularly unforgettable were those mesmerizing guarded eyes and that cryptic hypnotic smile.

She spoke only towards the end of the movie and her articulation was clear and precise, her diction and dialog delivery almost perfect. This part of the movie in which she finally revealed herself to be a real human person, she left an even deeper imprint than she did as the spurious apparition.

Memorable scenes

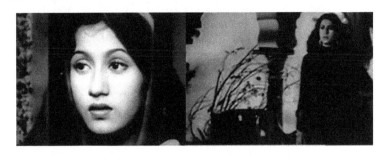

　　*Songs '...dil ne phir yaad kiya', '... mushkil hai bahut mushkil', '...hai mera dil', and of course the evergreen '...ayega aane wala'.
　　*Towards the end, the court scene (2: 04:25 - 2:13:05).
　　*The conversation between Madhubala and Ashok Kumar in the jail (2:13:55-2:19:40).

Apradhi

This movie was not exactly well-received at the popularity stakes but Madhubala was declared by most to be its only silver lining. It was certainly a decent movie though, admittedly, not the box office type. Critics praised her as mature and intelligent both in its lighthearted as well as intense portions. The way she executed the perfect 'mother' portrayal at the age of 16 also won her many accolades.

Memorable scenes

　　*The tete-a-tete between Madhubala and the hero when they run into each other inside a bus (10:00 - 12:00).
　　*Two beautiful songs, the '...jaan pehchan na, sahab salaam na', and the '...pyar karne walon ke liye hai duniya'.

6. Year 1950

This was another sumptuous year for Madhubala fans but three out of the half a dozen releases (Nishana, Madhubala and Hanste Aansoo) have completely gone missing. By this time, still a teenager, she had already been in the movie industry for several years and her confidence had grown considerably. None of her 1950 movies did a roaring business but Beqasoor, Pardes and Nirala were received well and her own performances won rich plaudits. Everything pointed to her having arrived big time. She was ardently sought after by public as well as the movie producers. The movie critics spoke admiringly of her as well.

Beqasoor

This was a charming movie and Madhubala carried it on her shoulders. Her smile, her innocence and her simplicity made her the indisputable darling of the masses. The movie did not call for extraordinary histrionics, only for her to be sweet, cuddly and lovable. She actually delivered a whole lot more. Whether it was her delicious dialog delivery or the singing and dancing of those melodious songs, she was like a fantasy come true.

Memorable scenes

*Madhubala's sweetness was simply overflowing throughout. We feel like picking the entire movie. For an easy way out, however, we are choosing these two beautiful songs '…aayee bhor suhani aayee', '… man men naachen man ki umangen', and the two gorgeous dance songs '…Hanske na teer chalaana' and '…akhiyan gulabi jaise mad ki hon pyalian'.

Pardes

In Pardes, Madhubala continued to wow her admirers with a charming exhibition of her comic genius, coming up, in the process, with another winning performance. How elegance, oomph and sex appeal when combined with genuine grace, poise and innocence can produce glorious spectacles is demonstrated in the song '…akhiyan milake zara baat karoji'. She was simply ravishing in appearance and electrifying in effect.

Memorable scenes

*Besides the song mentioned above, two other songs brought out Madhubala's genius in light and playful scenes - '…dheere dheere angna men aaja piya' and 'jiya laage nahin mora dekho ji sajan bin"

Nirala

Madhubala had so far been seen mostly in happy and humorous roles. She had provided glimpses of considerable proficiency in playing somber and tragic roles in movies like Mahal, Dulari and Apradhi (Madhubala's role in Mahal was rather grim and melancholy. Same can be said regarding parts of Apradhi and Dulari). But she left absolutely no doubts in Nirala, this aspect of her acting having been given full opportunity to blossom in its second half. She was compelling as the unhappy married woman whose grim and melancholy life ends in a suicide. In a magnificent display of versatility, she was also sparkling in the movie's first part in which she played a chipper and effervescent country girl. Although the movie itself had certain serious flaws and could manage only average pickings at the box office, Madhubala was, as always, persuasively impressive.

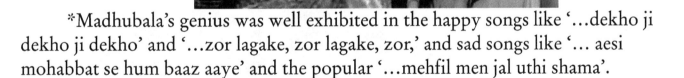

Memorable scenes

*Madhubala's genius was well exhibited in the happy songs like '…dekho ji dekho ji dekho' and '…zor lagake, zor lagake, zor,' and sad songs like '… aesi mohabbat se hum baaz aaye' and the popular '…mehfil men jal uthi shama'.

*Although the role of the bubbly irrepressible young girl was enchantingly played by Madhubala throughout the movies first half, my favorite sequence was when she fakes drowning (33:00- 36:50) and Dev Anand tries to treat her as a doctor.

7. Year 1951

By now, Madhubala had established herself as a major box office attraction but aside from Mahal, she had really not run into an exceptional script or movie. 1951 gave her one for the ages, Tarana. Like 1950, it was another productive year for

Madhubala in the sense that she acted in seven movies but three of them (Nazneen, Nadan and Khazana) receded into oblivion without raising as much as a ripple. Nadan had excellent music and the videos of a few of its songs are available, but not of the entire movie.

*The songs '…Aesa kya kasoor kiya dil jo', '…aa teri tasveer bana loon' and '…achha hota jo tu dil men' from Nadan are certainly worth a listen and watch.

Saiyan

This was a somewhat undistinguished adaptation of the magnificent 'Duel in the Sun' from Hollywood. Undistinguished because 'trying to wrap a Western body in an Indian soul' does not often work'. As an example, the erotic undertones and the sexual tension of the original had to be significantly watered down as they would not mesh with the Indian sensitivities of that day and age. Saiyan's producers also made no effort to try to emulate the original's stunning production values especially its gorgeous panoramas. As a result, the movie was not as compelling as 'Duel in the Sun'. Nevertheless, as a contemporary commentator said '… but it had Madhubala'. That says it all. She, and its musical score, were hard to forget. She acted well and looked out of this world.

Memorable Scenes

*All of its songs are worth watching. Definitely not an easy pick, here are some perennial favorites '….hawa men dil dole', '…kismet men khushi ka naam nahin', '…vo raat din, vo sham ki guzari' and 'kaali kaali raat re dil'.

*A fascinating sequence of the movie occurs when Madhubala walks back and forth trying to decide between the two verbally dueling brothers (1:02:30 - 1:03:10)

Tarana

In this movie Madhubala, still only 18 years old, was paired with Dilip Kumar, a celebrated actor with outstanding acting skills, who was also considerably more mature in age (28 years). The movie had a simple but pleasantly flowing storyline.

Dilip Kumar acted magnificently but Madhubala turned out to be its real star. We are not speaking here of just her fetching personality but even more so of her acting class. Outshining and outclassing Dilip Kumar was rare in Indian filmdom but Madhubala did it throughout the movie. In fact, she repeated it in every movie they acted together.

Memorable scenes

*It is impossible to choose. The whole movie and all its songs are immensely enjoyable and watching the whole movie is enthusiastically recommended. It should be readily available.

Badal

It was a run-of-the-mill movie with a pretty ordinary script. Even then Madhubala was unforgettable especially in lighthearted and comic scenes. It seemed so effortless for her to create magic with her flirtatious daintiness, her charming elegance and her sweet smiles. Prem Nath looked dashing as well, with its excellent musical score being another big plus.

Miscellaneous scenes

*Madhubala was exquisite in all the four songs which she was featured in. The duet '…ae dil na mujh se chhupa' was the most delectable. The happy song '…unse pyar ho gaya' and the sad ones '…do din ke liye mehman yahan' and '…rota hai mera dil' were viewing treats as well.

Aaram

Madhubala's character in this movie finds herself in an odd situation and the script demanded a sensitive understanding of its subtle nuances and a competent discharge of its requirements. Madhubala responded impeccably and did full justice to its awkward moments. No wonder she won kudos all across the board. The movie itself did not, however, do all that well.

Memorable scenes

　　*We can't think of too many extraordinary scenes in the movie but do feel that the songs '…man men kisee ki preet' and '…ae jaane jigar' were exquisitely elegant.

8. Year 1952

1952 saw three Madhubala movies. Sangdil - a decent production otherwise - simply was not the box office type while others failed to overcome their poor scripts and production values. Deshbhaktan disappeared without a trace, Saqi and Sangdil failing to bring down the house as well. Although Madhubala's performances were blemish-free, they were unable to pull these movies out of dross.

Saqi

This movie had nice music but was poorly written and poorly made. Madhubala played an Arab princess and was probably its only bright spot but her brightness failed to light up either the movie or the box office. The critics also could not find much to recommend it.

Memorable scenes

　　*This movie did not have a whole lot of memorable scenes. One interesting sequence was probably the one in which Madhubala demands from Prem Nath the proof of his love for her (1:51 - 1:55).

　　*The song '…aa gayi hai ishaq par bahar' was pleasant and popular but the lighting was too dark and its picturization far from scintillating.

Sangdil

Boasting great music and one of the most popular leading pairs of the day, the movie was another mediocre adaptation of a Western classic, Charlotte Brontë's Jane Eyre.

Madhubala and Dilip Kumar were both equally classy as far as acting is concerned but we can't help the feeling that Dilip Kumar and his eyes were just not half as expressive as Madhubala's and not only in this movie. Madhubala could clearly act, look and live her characters for more convincingly than Dilip Kumar could, in movie after movie.

We are not saying this lightly but after repeated viewings and diligent examination of Tarana, Sangdil, Amar and Mughal-e-Azam, the four movies in which the duo appeared together.

Memorable scenes

　　*Madhubala and Dilip Kumar appear in several conversational sequences in this movie, with wonderful dialogs being exchanged back and forth. Both of them excel but it is Madhubala whose image monopolizes the canvas of the viewer's mind long after the viewing is over.
　　*The popular songs '...dil men sama gaye sajan' and '...wo to chale gaye'.

9. Year 1953

Only two Madhubala movies made it to the theaters in 1953. While Armaan is nowhere to be found, a very poor and blurred copy of Rail Ka dibba is available.

Rail Ka Didda

This was an interesting movie with a novel idea but did not find favor with the viewing public. Madhubala was adorable as usual and acted with zest and assurance. But the role itself gave no scope for anything out of the ordinary.

Memorable scenes

　　*We love her form and energy in the song '...chhum chhama chhum payal baaje' and to a lesser extent '… paapi duniyan se door'. She lights up the whole screen with her spunk and sparkle.

10. Year 1954

The trend of box office success eluding Madhubala's movies continued for the third straight year with both the movies released this year not doing particularly well, although Amar was an excellent movie. Critics feel that Amar failed because it was well ahead of its time and that the public was not yet ready to accept its premise.

Bahut Din Hue

Bahut Din Huye was essentially a stunt movie based on a children's grandma folktale. Surely, a good movie can be made with illusion, magic, sorcery, grotesque characters and other fantasia but for that to happen a well told story and excellent special effects are a must, something that proved to be too tall an order for this movie. Madhubala touchingly portrayed an attractive village lass who became a queen to almost lose it all.

Memorable scenes

    * Madhubala delivered this beautiful song with classical elegance '…kyon chameli khilkhilati hai bataa'. The song has beautiful music and great poetry.
    * Another song '…chanda chamke neel gagan men' is also worth watching.
    * In one delightful interlude Madhubala and the hero of the movie converse with each other through the medium of a cow (47:45 – 49:32)

Amar

In spite of being a big banner film with good storyline, good direction, good performances and good music, the movie failed to ring in the cash registers. It did, however, give fillip to the evolving legend of Madhubala's acting artistry. Once again, she was paired with the acting proprietor of India's acting pinnacle Dilip Kumar, and once again she simply outclassed him, even though he gave a stellar performance of his own. This was no mean feat as every other actress of the time including the redoubtable Nargis, Meena Kumari and Vyjayanthimala found it hard to do so (in some movies they were decidedly as good as Dilip Kumar but none other than Madhubala surpassed him every time).

Both of them had complex roles in Amar but Madhubala's capability in expressing all their subtleties in just the right proportion and at just the right time was incredible. The reader is referred to chapter 3, section F (comparing Madhubala with her contemporaries) for a bit more on this.

Memorable scenes

In this movie Madhubala was amazing in practically every scene. It seems so unfair to be selective but how about the following –

* The songs '…na shikva hai koi', '…insaaf ka mandir hai yeh', '…mere sadke balam' and '…jaane waale se mulaqat na'
* And the two sequences, one when Nimmi refuses to get married at the wedding site (1:29:25 -1:32:02) and another when she comes to meet Madhubala at her house and Madhubala almost loses her own composure (2:00:20 - 2:03:46).

11. Year 1955

Teerandaaz and Naqab, out of the four Madhubala movies released in 1955 seem to have vanished altogether except for a few songs which can be heard without their associated videos. This year's other two movies would definitely find room in any list of Madhubala's dozen or so career-best although only one of them, Mr. and Mrs. 55, actuated a healthy jingle of money at the box office counters.

Naata

This movie, from Madhubala's own production house, was an artsy creation but probably was not expected to be lapped up by everyone, maybe not even by its makers. In line with her wont, however, Madhubala gave a magnificent account of herself as a simple, sensitive and affectionate girl who meets an adverse fate through gullibility and naiveté. The storyline, the production values, the performances and the music were of the highest caliber. It was like a poem on celluloid and is highly recommended for anyone with a yen for the offbeat and aesthetically superior movies.

Memorable scenes

* It was a heartwarming movie (despite its tragic ending) and Madhubala's performance was masterful throughout. Worth watching was the tremendously potent emoting by Madhubala in the happy songs '…mat samjho neer bahati hun', '… maujon ka ishara hai', '…lagan lagi hai, sajan milan ki' and the sad song '…dekhte dekhte jal gaya'.

* In this last song, the depth of agony portrayed by Madhubala without the melodrama was deeply stirring, in fact absolute stunning, a Madhubala special only she was capable of.

Mr. and Mrs. 55

That Mr. and Mrs. 55 is one of Madhubala's best ever movies has been affirmed by many people who should know, Dilip Kumar and Shammi Kapoor being only two of the instances.

This movie was a tremendous comedy - subtle, sophisticated and thoroughly enjoyable. While Guru Dutt, Johnny Walker, Lalita Pawar, Vinita Bhatt and Kumkum were all excellent, Madhubala was worlds beyond everyone else. She exhibited peerless histrionic abilities and easily eclipsed the others, her style, sense of timing, expressions and body language scaling the highest and the sublimest altitudes of prodigious acting.

Memorable scenes

Mr. and Mrs. 55 was another one of those movies in which it is impossible to choose or limit oneself to bits and pieces because in every scene that Madhubala makes an appearance, she leaves an equally indelible imprint. If we must, however, here are some of the movie's perennially regarded scenes.

* For their comic value, the scenes at the tennis courts when she accidentally drops her shoes on Guru Dutt's face (6: 37 - 8:40); in the park with her lady servant where she finds Guru Dutt sitting on a bench and they get into a conversation (54:10 -57:35); the whole sequence in which both of them run into each other outside the office of the registrar of marriages and her making the shocking discovery soon afterwards of who her groom was really going to be (1:04:09 - 1:09:00).

* For its dramatic value, the entire episode surrounding the song '…neele aasmani' (1:11:39 - 1:19:12).

* For an almost perfect depiction of love and passion by Madhubala in the most refined and elegant way possible, watch the song '…udhar tum hasin ho' (1:43:26 - 1:48:15). There is nothing brazen or even overt but every gesture, every body movement and every quiver of Madhubala's facial muscles oozes aroused love and sexual tension. She almost seems to be sweating, without actually doing so. Nothing even remotely comparable to this performance has ever been seen from any other actor or actress - at least not in Indian movies.

12. Year 1956

This year two of Madhubala movies saw moderate success at the box office but the third, Dhake Ki Malmal proved to be flop and is not available now. She played princesses in both the others and looked and acted every bit like one. The movies were not particularly well-made or entertaining. That did not, by any means, stop Madhubala from giving supremely capable and engagingly competent performances aided sumptuously, of course, by her lavish beauty and heavenly smiles.

Raj Hath

As a Rajput princess caught in a drama of familial vengeance, she was like a balm in the general theater of ennui. On fluent display was the superb Madhubala artistry and so was the continuing tradition of her heart stealing ways.

Memorable scenes

* Two truly enjoyable songs of this movie to which Madhubala's presence added much luster, were '...mere sapne men aana re sajna' and '...yeh vaada karo chand ke saamne'. In the beginning of the former song, her manner of looking back and flashing a sheepish smile at a companion who was watching her is so endearing that it won her millions of admirers. It's remarkable how she could get the style and form of these little gestures so impeccably perfect.

*The delightful episode in which, Madhubala goes to Pardeep Kumar's tent with the intention to killing him but ends up falling for his chivalry and humanity instead (1:13:28 -1:17:48).

Shirin Farhad

This movie was the somberly made version of a traditional love story with grim outcome. As its lovesick heroine, a Persian princess, whose family marry her away to someone other than the man she loves, Madhubala portrayed the tragic girl with just the precise amount of lovely elegance and serene dispiritedness. Both she and Pardeep Kumar, its hero, won praise for their work but a movie with almost constant melancholia requires an exceptional screenplay to make it digestible. Unfortunately for this movie, such succor was not forthcoming. As a result, neither its two actors nor its popular musical score could manage to dig it out of its morass of mediocrity.

Memorable scenes

For a movie without particularly memorable scenes, it did certainly have great songs. We mention just a few here - the haunting '...guzraa hua zamana aata nahin', the melodious '...ae dilruba jaane wafa' and the touching '...aaja O jaane wafa'.

13. Year 1957

1957 saw the release of 3 Madhubala movies - the now unavailable Yahudi Ki Ladki and the modestly successful Gateway of India and Ek Saal. By now a well-established star, her performances could always be expected to be of the highest caliber and in Gateway of India, in particular, she virtually touched the skies.

Gateway of India

Not without flaws, this movie achieved breathtaking production values in some respects. One of the first woman dominated movies in India, it pitched Madhubala against six male actors, her encounter with each presenting a different scenario and requiring unique but multifaceted responses from Madhubala. Thanks to the way she aced each one of them displaying distinctive behavioral patterns and lingoes in the process, it came out to be extremely watchable and very enjoyable. Like Amar, this movie was said to be too far ahead of its time. That may have been responsible for the tepid response to it at the box office but Madhubala's own performance was supreme and did full justice to her status as a quality actress at the zenith of her art.

Memorable scenes

One has to see the whole movie to follow the context but a few of the following sequences may be enjoyable even in isolation.

 * When Madhubala cons Chander Shekhar into becoming her partner in a spurious scheme (35:25 - 39:30)
 * When she feigns drunkenness with Johnny Walker (49:50 - 55:56). This sequence includes the song '…dekhta chala gaya main'.
 * When Om Parkash threatens her with a knife and the exchange between them right afterwards (1:27:58 - 1:34:10)
 * The song '…do ghadi wo jo pas aa baithe (1:41:56)'.

Ek Saal

Though a little simplistic at times, Ek Saal had something special. Despite all the cheating and thuggery at the core of its story, it still felt like a tale of lyrical love, Madhubala being its most lyrical component as she played a gentle and refined heiress of delicate looks and the most lovable of comportments. Her character was too good to be real but she made it so believable and melted every heart with her honest and sensitive portrayal.

Memorable scenes

    * These three songs will probably be a representative sample of this movies lilting tenor - '…chale bhi aao, tumhe kasam hai (23:50), '…chhum chhum chali piya ki gali (34:06)' and '…sab kuchh luta ke (the female version at 1:57:10)'.

14. Year 1958

Madhubala had six movies in 1958. No one is sure what made an actress of her caliber and eminence to accept movies like Baghi Sipahi and Police. Both of them made their unceremonious exits from theater screens almost as soon as they showed up. Baghi Sipahi is not even available now. Police does have some copies available but the prints are horrible. The videos are blurry and the audios worse. It is hard to sit through these blemished copies but enough is visible to tell why the movie bombed at the box office and why the critics excoriated it.

The remaining 4 movies were decidedly better and restored Madhubala's status as a box office magnet, 1958 actually proving to be one of Madhubala's best ever years.

Police

It was brave of Madhubala to have taken this role. It is possible that she took it as a lark for she played a modern siren with vampish, flirtatious dresses and demeanor, something the mainstream Indian actresses of those days zealously avoided. It was a measure of Madhubala's confidence that she could hazard such an outlandish role but she seemed to be enjoying it as can be seen in the three songs below.

Memorable scenes

    * Though the movie itself was rather forgettable, the video clips of some of its songs do wow and enthrall if only because they show a different side of our most treasured icon. Here are three such songs '…chale hum kahan kaho', '…dil men hamare chhup ja' and '…o o o o baby'. In the first of these songs she looks ethereally beautiful, in the second and third riveting.

Phagun

Phagun was a delicious entertainer, Madhubala and its music being its biggest draws. The audience watched her completely mesmerized as she sang and danced her way into their hearts (the dances by themselves were not of the highest quality but a dancing Madhubala could be a feast in its own right). People called her Baazigar Jadugarni (the Gypsy wizard) as her character in the movie was that of a Gypsy girl and compared her with Mohini, a female incarnation of Lord Vishnu, who could seduce any man. The movie, as the reader might have guessed, became a resounding success.

Memorable scenes

* Madhubala had many enchanting dance songs in this movie each of them worth viewing. Here are some - '…teer yeh chhupke chalaya kisne', '…piya piya na laage mora jiya', '…ik pardesi mera dil' and '...chhum chhum ghugroo baaje'.
* Her acting adroitness is most visible in the song '…main soya akhiyan meeche'. Her expressions were so precise as to be typical and exceptional at the same time. Many critics commented that she was 'simply magical' in this song.
* An interesting sequence occurs when she goes to rescue her lover from the mean princess who is holding him and gets into an energetic scuffle with her (1:34:10 - 1:38:00).

Kala Pani

If Madhubala was a wizard in Phagun, she was almost divine in Kala Pani. It was a movie in which both, she and her hero Dev Anand , gave scintillating performances. So did the beautiful Nalini Jaywant, another celebrated heart stealer of Indian movies.

Memorable scenes

* The delightfully upbeat conversation at lunch table where she is introduced

to Dev Anand (27:50 - 30:34)

* The meeting between Madhubala and Dev Anand on the roof of her house, during which they express their love for each other (59:50 - 1:03:13) is simply delightful. The manner in which Madhubala displays her attraction for Dev Anand, her eyes glistening with love, desire, wistfulness and partially suppressed passion all cresting at the same time is unparalleled and unmatched by any other Indian actor, male or female.

* Her show of indignation and outrage at Dev Anand after having seen him visiting a house of ill repute (1:27:25 - 1:28:45), is a testimonial to her inordinately adept acting skills.

* The entire sequence in which she tries to placate and reconcile with a resentful Dev Anand (1:34:52 - 1:43:52) and includes the most enchanting and insanely popular song '…achha ji main haari chalo' is what the legends are made of. It is definitely a must see.

Howrah Bridge

In this movie, Madhubala came up with another towering performance. It was unique and extraordinary for several reasons. She played a sophisticated but sweet and simpleminded Anglo-Indian hotel singer. Required to be contemporary and traditional at the same time, she also had to speak an unusual dialect and to dance to orchestra songs, something the contemporary mainstream actresses were not used to be doing. She accepted the challenge and did it with, oh, such oomph and spirit. Orchestra songs of those days were like the 'Item songs' of today and Madhubala made a couple of them immortal in this movie. But unlike the present times, she did it fully clothed and without any indecent or vulgar gestures or maneuvers while still looking ravishingly seductive.

Memorable scenes

* Two orchestra songs, the timeless '…aaiye meherban', and the catchy '…dekhe teri nazar'. These songs were not a celebration of her dancing skills (although her body did have a seductive sensuous rhythm of its own) but even more of her dexterity at communicating inner feelings through facial expressions and body language that immortalized these songs. Constantly in a close up mode, we are sure

that even the cameras were absolutely thrilled.

   * Two other must-see songs displaying Madhubala's ethereal beauty and her enactment of pure love and contentment are '…yeh kya kar dala toone' (1:08:48 – 1:13:42 includes her short conversation with Ashok Kumar just prior to the song) and '…muhabbat ka haath javani ka palla'.

Chalti Ka Naam Gaadi

Chalti Ka Naan Gaadi completed the quartet of splendid movies from Madhubala that did extremely well at the box office in 1958. Her own performance in this movie also won millions of hearts.

Although the movie degenerated into a murder mystery towards its end, its major premise and the prime reason for its success was its comic core. With comedy adepts like Madhubala and Kishore Kumar as its leading pair, it had the perfect ingredients to make it memorable. While Kishore Kumar had a tendency towards the loud and the slapstick, Madhubala's comedy was, as always, subtle, elegant and restrained. It was, as ever, her natural flair, her superb timing and her exhilarating presence that won her the richest ovations.

Memorable scenes

Madhubala was stunning in every scene but we mention only a few here. Another thing, it was a good movie to watch for her lilting intoxicating laugh which, as someone said, could 'wake up even a corpse'. The following words from Satyen Bose, her director in this movie say it so well '… Unabashed mirth, laughter pristine and infectious'.

   * The banter between Madhubala and her friend after Madhubala's father brings up a marriage proposal for her (1:12:15 - 1:13:30).
   * When, chased as a thief, Kishore Kumar inadvertently ends up in Madhubala's bedroom (39:50 - 43:20).
   * When Madhubala shows up at Kishore Kumar's garage to pay her unpaid bill (1:13:57 - 1:20:08).
   * Some delightful songs - '…haal kaisa hai janab ka', '…ek ladki bheegi bhagi

si', '…mai sitaron ka taraana' and '…ruk jao na ji'

15. Year 1959

The symptoms of Madhubala's physical ailment were getting worse by this time although she appeared to cope well and came up with three movies. None of them can be considered exceptional although Madhubala herself refused to be weighed down by their mediocrity. In Insaan Jaag Utha in particular, she was simply marvelous. One must understand, however, that she did not have to be exceptional to be impressive. Excellent acting simply ran in her blood and she could be exceptional without breaking a sweat.

Kal Hamara Hai

A fairly feeble movie, its story and the screenplay were rather contrived, its director not seeming to be sure about what to do with it.

Madhubala played the only double role of her life in this movie, that of twin sisters, one totally unlike the other in every respect. Although the gentle sister's role must have been a walk in the park for Madhubala, her role as the ultramodern and westernized but immature and impulsive other sister was not only unusual for her but also entirely antithetical of her public image. Not all her fans were happy to see her as this second character but that her acting was of the finest grade is not contested by anyone. Her interpretation of the role was immaculate and many critics and journalists wrote plaudits on her performance.

Memorable scenes

 * The meeting between the 'good sister' and Bharat Bhushan on the roof of her house (42:50 - 45:15).
 * The series of sequences involving the 'bad sister', during which she encounters Jayant and negotiates a deal (1:04:33 - 1:09:30).
 * The song '…aa aa meri taal pe naach le babu' (51:30).

Insaan Jaag Utha

This movie had two distinct themes. Both ran simultaneously but the crime portion was not very well written, proving to be a drag on the entire movie. The other component was, however, much more riveting. This portion consisted of a stirringly filmed love story which was soothing, sweet and thrilling, all at the same time. Madhubala, played a poor but upright construction worker who was delicate, sensitive and graceful but also tenacious and resolute. Madhubala's performance was transcended everything else though Sunil Dutt's was delightful as well.

Memorable scenes

* When Sunil Dutt comes to Madhubala's home for a cup of tea (26:35 - 31:15).
* The song '...baat badhti gayi' and her conversation with Sunil Datt just prior to it (57:38 - 1:03:41). Only Madhubala could generate such exhilaration and romantic energy.
* This movie has a remarkable scene demonstrating Madhubala's versatility in portraying all emotions effectively. This time it was anger. The incident happens after she sees Sunil Dutt dancing with another girl (1:23:38 - 1:24:38).
* The song '...chand sa mukhra kyon sharmaya', is one of the most enchanting romantic love songs in Indian movies. Sunil Dutt was debonair but Madhubala was simply goddess incarnate. She was ravishing, as always, to look at but it was her love-laden eyes, her honey-dripping facial expressions and her sensuous body movements that raised this song to a cult status.

Do Ustad

It was a drab crime drama whose major plus was Madhubala's sunny exhilarating presence and her dynamic performance. Another was its catchy music and interesting song sequences. But its underlying inanity had no trouble in sinking the movie.

Memorable scenes

    * This movie had exciting music but was bereft of many memorable scenes. Most of its songs were quite entertaining and provocative - '…nazron ke teer maare kas kas kas', '…hum pe dil aaya to bolo kya karoge', '…ruk ruk ruk kahan chali deewani', '…tu ladki main ladka', and '…rik rik tik tik, boom boom chik' but our favorite remains '…aaya tum pe dil aaya'.

16. Year 1960

This was the year in which Madhubala's medical evaluations in England uncovered the seriousness of her heart ailment, pronouncing the grave prognosis of a mere two years of life expectancy. She continued to work bravely, however, at the cost of significant physical and mental strain, though, fortunately for her, her professional life proved less taxing and continued to ring in triumphs. It brought her massive appreciation and long overdue recognition. Madhubala had four movies released this year, two of them (Mughal-e-Azam and Barsaat Ki Raat) proving to be blockbusters and inspiring glowing panegyrics by all and sundry not only to her sublime beauty but also to her acting acumen. The other two (Mehlon Ke Khwab and Jaali Note) turned out to be merely also rans.

Mehlon Ke Khwab

This movie was another home production for Madhubala (we already talked about Naata, of the year 1955). It was a full-length comedy, with a minor crime angle and more than a touch of slapstick. The first half was cute, the movie losing some of its charm in the second half. The fact that Madhubala and her real life sister Chanchal were both delightfully entertaining and alluringly attractive failed to overcome its other shortcomings and it fizzled unceremoniously at the box office.

Memorable scenes

    * The early parts of the movie in which the two girls discuss their lives and their options followed by their escape from their humdrum lives are quite absorbing and stimulating especially the song '…is duniyan men sabse achhi cheez'.

Jaali Note

An average crime drama with fairly average production values, this movie did nothing that could take the world by storm. Madhubala, on the other hand, did leave a pretty favorable impression. She was, by no means, unforgettable or exceptional in this movie, but her fans came out quite strongly in the expression of their adorations of her.

Memorable scenes

* The song '… Such kehta hoon bahut haseen ho' easily qualifies as being memorable. Two other songs were entertaining as well - "…dil hai aapka hazoor' and "… chand zard zard hai'. Her makeup was, perhaps, overdone in some scenes.

Mughal-e Azam

If ever a proof was needed of Madhubala having no parallels in Indian Cinema as an actress and as an artist, Mughal-e-Azam provided it with a bang. Even though her performances in movies like Mahal, Tarana, Amar, Mr & Mrs 55, Insaan Jaag Utha and even Naata, Kala Paani, Beqasoor, Howrah Bridge, Sangdil and Gateway of India were no less classy and the authenticity of Madhubala's position amongst the topmost was never a subject of question or uncertainty, Mughal-e-Azam provided the final stamp of authority. This movie, made with great effort and dedication, had quality gushing out of its every pore, Madhubala being, without doubt, the finest of its exhibits.

Memorable scenes

Madhubala was marvelous in almost every scene she was part of. We mention only a few here but highly recommend that the whole movie be seen to appreciate Madhubala's acting genius and her incomparable beauty.

* The two immortal songs – '…pyar kiya to darna kya' and '…mohe panghat pe nandlal chhed gyo re'.

* The ultra-romantic and well-known feather scene, which became famous despite Dilip Kumar, the male counterpart of the romantic pair, remaining utterly stone-faced throughout the scene (and the movie).

* Madhubala's many encounters with Prithviraj Kapoor, the veteran actor with a dominating personality, and one of the many acting stalwarts in the movie.

Barsaat Ki Raat

Madhubala played an innocent, sweet and well-bred girl. Her performance was bright, lively and dignified. She looked and acted like a dream, the public loving her easy poise and relaxed naturalness. Some scenes succinctly revealed her canny ability to read and display human emotions and portray them with exemplary adroitness.

Memorable scenes

* A cherished scene from this movie was the one which gave it its title. The stormy night when Madhubala walks into the shelter of an ironsmith's shed was immortalized simply by Madhubala's arousing presence. The lightning from the sky was not half as spine tingling as the rain drenched physical appeal she exuded and the facial expressions she displayed (15:20 - 16:36).

* A sweeter than honey look and a trance-like portrayal of infatuated bliss was brought to life by Madhubala in the songs '…zindagi bhar nahin bhoolegi' (especially the male version) and '…maine shayad tumhen pehle bhi kahin'.

17. Year 1961

Madhubala died in 1969 but her last movie was released in 1971. In the last decade or so of her life, six of her movies were released.

All these movies were affected by the production issues that had to do with Madhubala's unfortunate medical condition. Although the diagnosis had been known for a while, the full implications of its extent and grave prognosis were not fully appreciated until 1960 when she visited England and received a a full medical work up. Her death was predicted to ensue within the next couple of years. It can easily be imagined what kind of effect it might have had on a 27 year-old girl and how life must have changed for one who, till the other day, was in the prime of her life and on the top of the universe.

Nevertheless, she carried on courageously and tried to keep up the appearances. But some of the things could not simply be wished away. First, her deteriorating health made it impossible for her to complete a few of her movies. Many others took an extraordinarily long time, sometimes even requiring the use of doubles and, in worst cases, of massive editing. Second, thin wisps of gloom and despair could occasionally be identified behind those expressive eyes. Her luminescent smile and her free-spirited laugh too had some of the jingle squeezed out of them although, it must be admitted that, the consummate actress that she was, it was impossible to tell most of the time.

Of the six movies made during this period, three were released in the year of 1961. They were all decent but average movies and none displayed a huge box office potential.

Passport

This was a run-of-the-mill crime drama which failed to impress. This statement does not, of course, apply to Madhubala's performance. She sparkled like a gem and was exquisite as usual. It is incredible how, even in terribly done movies, she could find ways to hit the bull's-eye.

Memorable scenes

* Some enjoyable scenes (13:50 - 27:20) show a dazzlingly vivacious Madhubala as her car breaks down and include the song '…sun le dastan'.
* The song '…saaz-e-dil chhed de' illustrates how effective Madhubala could be in romantic sequences with angelic looks, dreamy eyes and seductive smiles. In this respect, this song almost matches those three others in the romantic genre - '…chand sa mukhra kyon sharmaya' from Insaan Jaag Utha, '…main soya akhiyan meeche' from Phagun and '…ae dil na mujhse chhupa' from Badal.

Jhumroo

Despite its rough edges, most of the time it was a mellow love story. Kishore Kumar, Lalita Pawar and Chanchal were all very good but it was Madhubala, who as the life of its soulful story, left everyone captivated. Only she could score such sensitive performances without being stagy. The rough edges I mentioned above, however, did not allow this movie to rise above the humdrum category.

Memorable scenes

Madhubala looked gorgeous and remarkably convincing in an unconvincing story. She was appealing and memorable in every scene she appeared. Such scenes were, however, scattered all over the entire movie. Here are a few that the viewer may enjoy.

* The happy version of the song '…Thandi hava ye chaandni suhaani' and Madhubala's conversation with Anoop Kumar immediately following the song. The sad version of this song was equally good.
* The comic interlude following which she ends up singing a song with Kishore Kumar and Anoop Kumar (52:10 - 57:30). The song is '…jhoome re, jhoome re, jhoome'.
* The sequence in which her father threatens and orders her to decline marriage with Kishore Kumar and she goes down the stairs to have a chat with him (1:54:20 - 1:57:50).

Boyfriend

A little sadness seems to have crept in uninvited behind those beautiful eyes in some scenes of this movie. Perhaps they were shot soon after her medical prognosis was revealed to her. Or may be it is just an over-reading by some viewers. Her

character in the movie was, after all, meant to be pensive and ruminative.

Memorable scenes

Not too many scenes in this movie could be described as particularly noteworthy but the following were interesting.

    * The song '…aigo aigo yeh kya ho gya'.
    * The whole sequence of scenes in which Madhubala finds out that the necklace she is wearing has been stolen (1:29:30 – 1:30:41).
    * When the Thakur goes to the sisters with his proposal that Madhubala start working again (1:58:38 - 2:01: 26).

18. Year 1962

This year saw only one release from the now famous Venus of India. New offers were drying up as well since the news of her illness had been spreading and become common knowledge by now.

Half Ticket

This movie did good business at the box office due not only to Madhubala's energetic, alluring, enchanting and charismatic comedy which never did, of course, cross the limits of plausibility but also on account of Kishore Kumar's boisterous and slapstick buffoonery which, though entirely over the top, was fancied and enjoyed by many. If she looked a little sad in the movie Boy Friend, movies like Jhumroo and Half Ticket seemed to have brought her smile and mojo back. Compellingly charming in both, nothing suggested anything was amiss.

Memorable scenes

    * A couple of songs of this movie definitely made a splash. Both Madhubala and Kishore Kumar were cute, entertaining, likable and even adorable in – '…chand raat tum ho saath' and '…aankhon men tum'.
    * The scene in the train in which Madhubala meets Kishore Kumar disguised as a mentally challenged youth (39:00 - 45:18) was humorous.

* The scene in which Kishore Kumar fakes suicidal intentions (1:27:32 - 1:29:19) was cute though not very well done.

19. Year 1964

Only one of Madhubala's movies showed up on the cinema screens in 1964 and that too after a complete miss in 1963. As an actress Madhubala was already fading from the public view and mind.

Sharabi

This movie did not set the proverbial rivers on fire but Madhubala was still glorious and looked tantalizingly alluring, leaving her mark as an actress as well. So did her male counterpart Dev Anand, but the movie lacked the cinematic essentials of box office success and it showed.

Memorable scenes

　　　* Two songs '…tum ho hasin kahan ke' and '…jao ji jao dekhe hain bare'. The first one, in particular, showed that Madhubala had not lost any of her charm, beauty, sensuality and 'adas'.
　　　* The scene in which Dev Anand comes home and his little sister gets injured with the resultant ruckus in(1:33:48 - 1:36:10).

20. Year 1971

1971 saw the release of Madhubala's last ever movie Jwaala, seven years after the release of her previous one in 1964 (Sharabi) and two years after she had already departed from this mortal world.

Jwaala

This, Madhubala's first full-length feature film in color, also proved to be her last. Some of its shooting was done around or before 1960 but many parts had to be completed later, either during Madhubala's sickness or after her death, using doubles. Whatever the merits or the demerits of the movie itself, it gave her innumerable fans the opportunity to see her radiant beauty, her luscious lips and her delicate complexion enhanced and made more lustrous and enchanting by the addition of color. To see her perfect figure wrapped in saris of gorgeous pastel hues was another treat that made this movie worth a watch.

Memorable scenes

* These 3 songs are a real treat for the eyes but the viewer has to watch for the occasional 'double' masquerading as Madhubala – "…dekho ji, aankh men dekho', '…aaja re aaja, more sajan aa' and '…jaagi raat bhar'.

Chapter 6: Ranking Madhubala's Movies and Performances

Ranking anything is a slippery slope and by its very nature arbitrary. We have spoken to many people but eventually we own full responsibility for putting the order on the rankings. We understand that not everyone will agree with or find them consonant with his or her taste. We assure the reader that we have, on our part, done our best to be just and unbiased.

The we were should keep in mind that these rankings apply only to those movies which were available.

Note: The rankings are in a descending order.

Ranking of Madhubala's own performances

A. Sublime –

1. Mughal-e-Azam
2. Mr. and Mrs. 55
3. Tarana
4. Amar
5. Kala Paani
6. Insaan Jaag Utha
7. Chalti Ka Naam Gaadi
8. Mahal
9. Naata
10. Sangdil
11. Howrah Bridge
12. Barsaat Ki Raat

B. Distinguished –

1. Gateway of India
2. Ek Saal

3. Phagun
4. Beqasoor
5. Nirala
6. Singaar
7. Saiyan
8. Apradhi
9. Dil Ki Rani
10. Jhumroo

C. Excellent –

1. Mehlon Ke Khwaab
2. Aaram
3. Neel Kamal
4. Pardes
5. Kal Hamara Hai
6. Rajhath
7. Sharabi
8. Do Ustad
9. Passport
10. Rail Ka Dibba

D. Good –

1. Shirin Farhad
2. Badal
3. Dulari
4. Bahut Din Hue
5. Jaali Note
6. Half-Ticket
7. Jwaala
8. Boyfriend
9. Basant
10. Saqi

Ranking of Madhubala's best 16 movies in terms of their quality and watch worthiness

1. Mr. and Mrs. 55
2. Mughal-e-Azam
3. Tarana
4. Kala Paani
5. Amar
6. Chalti Ka Naam Gaadi
7. Barsaat Ki Raat
8. Mahal
9. Howrah Bridge
10. Insaan Jaag Utha
11. Gateway of India
12. Phagun
13. Beqasoor
14. Naata
15. Sangdil
16. Dil Ki Rani

Ranking of Madhubala's best romantic songs (along with movie names)

1. Chand sa mukhra kyon sharmaya - Insaan Jaag Utha
2. Achha ji main haari chalo - Kalapaani
3. Ae dil na mujhse chhupa - Badal
4. Beiman tore nainva nindiya na aaye - Tarana
5. Main soya akhiyan meeche - Phagun
6. Akhiyan milake zara baat karojee - Pardes
7. Saaz-e-dil chhed de - Passport
8. Nain mile nain hue baawre - Tarana
9. Chanda re tu meri gawahi - Singaar
10. Yeh kya kar dala tune - Howrah Bridge
11. Dekho ji, aankh men dekho - Jwaala
12. Dil men sama gaye sajan - Sangdil

Ranking of Madhubala's best screen characters

1. As Gauri in Insaan Jaag Utha
2. As Tarana in Tarana
3. As Anju in Amar
4. As Asha in KalaPani
5. As Usha in Beqasoor
6. As Anarkali in Mughal-e- Azam
7. As Renu in Chalti Ka Naam Gaadi
8. As Tara in Naata
9. As Edna in Howrah Bridge
10. As Anju in Gateway of India
11. As Kamala in Sangdil
12. As Banani in Phagun
13. As Shabnam in Barsaat Ki Raat

CPSIA information can be obtained
at www.ICGtesting.com
Printed in the USA
BVHW012146171019
561451BV00003B/58/P